The NFL's Greatest Teams

NEW ENGLAND PATRIOTS

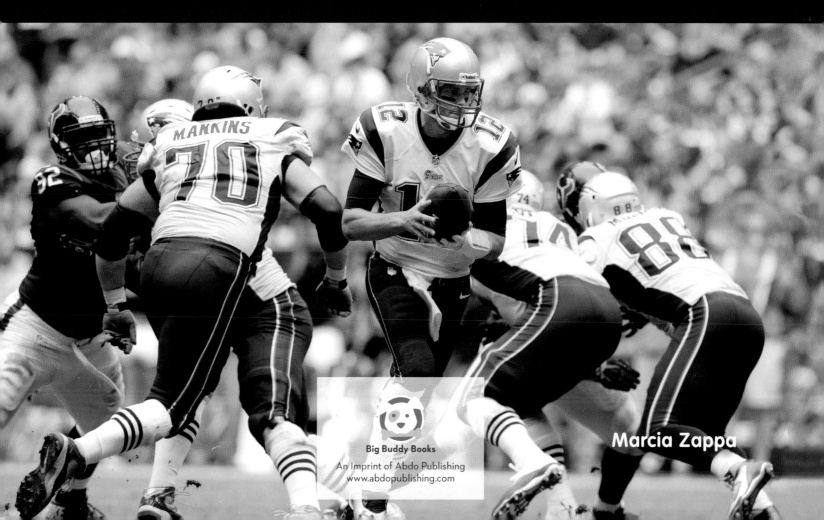

Big Buddy Books
An Imprint of Abdo Publishing
www.abdopublishing.com

Marcia Zappa

www.abdopublishing.com

Published by Abdo Publishing, a division of ABDO, PO Box 398166, Minneapolis, Minnesota 55439.
Copyright © 2015 by Abdo Consulting Group, Inc. International copyrights reserved in all countries. No part of this book may be reproduced in any form without written permission from the publisher. Big Buddy Books™ is a trademark and logo of Abdo Publishing.

Printed in the United States of America, North Mankato, Minnesota.
042014
092014

Cover Photo: ASSOCIATED PRESS.
Interior Photos: ASSOCIATED PRESS (pp. 5, 7, 11, 13, 14, 15, 17, 18, 19, 20, 21, 23, 25, 27, 28, 29); Getty Images (pp. 9, 19, 20).

Coordinating Series Editor: Rochelle Baltzer
Contributing Editors: Bridget O'Brien, Sarah Tieck
Graphic Design: Michelle Labatt

Library of Congress Cataloging-in-Publication Data

Zappa, Marcia, 1985-
 New England Patriots / Marcia Zappa.
    pages cm. -- (The NFL's greatest teams)
  ISBN 978-1-62403-363-6
1. New England Patriots (Football team)--History--Juvenile literature. I. Title.
  GV956.N36Z37 2015
  796.332'640974461--dc23
                        2013046916

Contents

A Winning Team

The New England Patriots are a football team in the National Football League (NFL). They are based in Massachusetts. But, they are the home team for all the New England states.

The Patriots have had good seasons and bad. Over time, they've become one of the NFL's greatest teams.

Blue, silver, red, and white are the team's colors.

Time Out

New England includes Massachusetts, Connecticut, Maine, New Hampshire, Rhode Island, and Vermont.

5

League Play

The NFL got its start in 1920. Its teams have changed over the years. Today, there are 32 teams. They make up two conferences and eight divisions.

The Patriots play in the Eastern Division of the American Football Conference (AFC). This division also includes the Buffalo Bills, the Miami Dolphins, and the New York Jets.

Team Standings

The AFC and the National Football Conference (NFC) make up the NFL. Each conference has a north, south, east, and west division.

The New York Jets have long been a rival of the Patriots.

Tom Brady helped the Patriots win three Super Bowls.

Kicking Off

The team started out in Boston in 1960. They were one of the first teams in the American Football League (AFL). The team was owned by a group of businessmen led by William H. "Billy" Sullivan Jr.

At first, the team was called the Boston Patriots. In 1970, the AFL joined the NFL. The next year, the team moved to a nearby city. So, they changed their name to the New England Patriots.

Patriots refers to Americans who fought in the Revolutionary War. Many events of this war took place in Boston.

Highlight Reel

The Patriots didn't stand out during their early years. They played in the AFL **championship** game in 1963. They didn't make it to the play-offs again until 1976. In 1986, they played in their first Super Bowl!

In 1993, the team hired coach Bill Parcells. And, they **drafted** quarterback Drew Bledsoe. Parcells and Bledsoe led the team back to the Super Bowl in 1997.

Win or Go Home

NFL teams play 16 regular season games each year. The teams with the best records are part of the play-off games. Play-off winners move on to the conference championship. Then, conference winners face off in the Super Bowl!

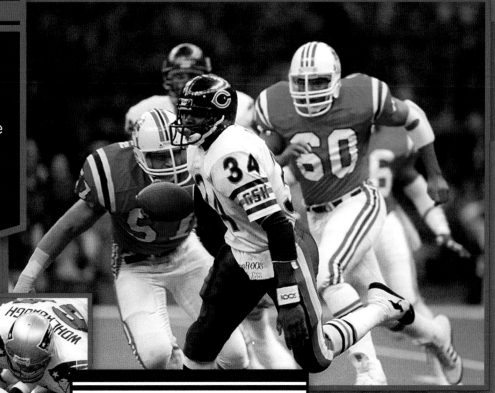

The Patriots lost their first two Super Bowls. In 1986, the Chicago Bears won 46–10 (*above*). In 1997, the Green Bay Packers won 35–21 (*left*).

Touchdown!

In 2007, the Patriots broke many NFL single-season records. This included most points scored and most touchdowns.

In 2000, Bill Belichick and Tom Brady joined the team. They led the Patriots to their first Super Bowl win in 2002! They beat the Saint Louis Rams 20–17.

The team was becoming stronger. They won the Super Bowl again in 2004 and 2005.

In 2007, the Patriots had the best regular season in NFL history. They won all 16 games and made it to the Super Bowl. But, they lost to the New York Giants 17–14. They lost again to the Giants in the 2012 Super Bowl.

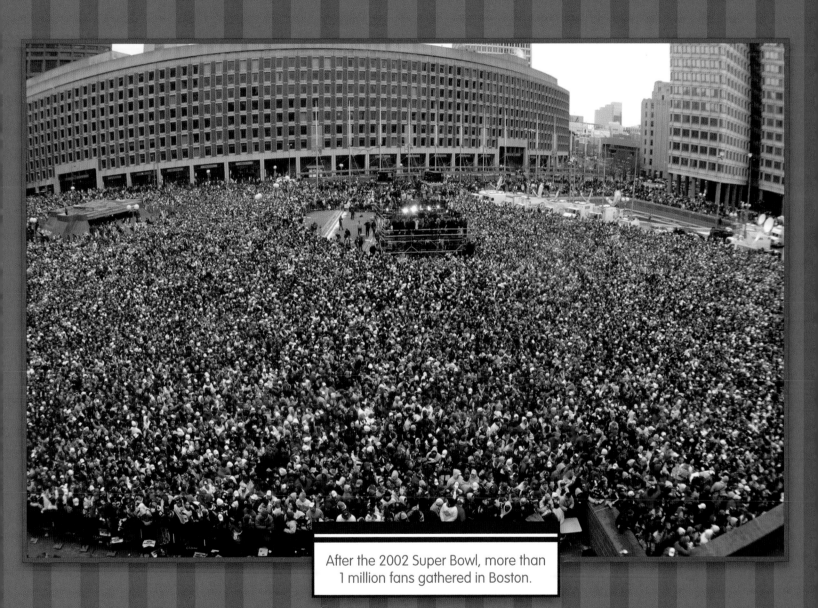

After the 2002 Super Bowl, more than 1 million fans gathered in Boston.

Halftime! Stat Break

Pro Football Hall of Famers & Their Years with the Patriots

Nick Buoniconti, Linebacker (1962–1968)
John Hannah, Guard (1973–1985)
Mike Haynes, Cornerback (1976–1982)
Andre Tippett, Linebacker (1982–1993)

Fan Fun

STADIUM: Gillette Stadium
LOCATION: Foxborough, Massachusetts
MASCOT: Pat Patriot

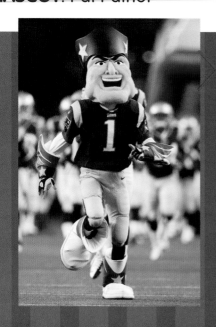

Team Records

RUSHING YARDS
Career: Sam Cunningham, 5,453 yards (1973–1982)
Single Season: Corey Dillon, 1,635 yards (2004)
PASSING YARDS
Career: Tom Brady, 49,149 yards
    and gaining (2000–)
Single Season: Tom Brady, 5,235 yards (2011)
RECEPTIONS
Career: Wes Welker, 672 receptions (2007–2012)
Single Season: Wes Welker, 123 receptions (2009)
ALL-TIME LEADING SCORER
Adam Vinatieri, 1,158 points (1996–2005)

Famous Coaches

Bill Parcells (1993–1996)
Bill Belichick (2000–)

Championships

SUPER BOWL APPEARANCES:
1986, 1997, 2002, 2004, 2005,
2008, 2012

SUPER BOWL WINS:
2002, 2004, 2005

Coaches' Corner

In 1993, Bill Parcells took over a struggling team. Already a successful NFL coach, he turned the Patriots around.

In 2000, Bill Belichick became the team's coach. In 2002, he led the team to its first Super Bowl win! Several strong seasons followed.

Teamwork

Belichick was part of Parcells's coaching staff with the Patriots, the Jets, and the Giants.

Parcells was only the second NFL coach to lead two different teams to the Super Bowl.

Belichick has been named Coach of the Year three times.

Star Players

Gino Cappelletti
WIDE RECEIVER/KICKER
(1960–1970)

Gino Cappelletti is known as the "original Patriot." He played for the team during its first ten years. In 1964, he was named the AFL's Most Valuable Player (MVP). He scored 1,130 points during his **career**. That was more than any other player in the AFL. Until 2005, that was more than any other Patriot.

John Hannah GUARD (1973–1985)

John Hannah was a powerful member of the team's offensive line. In 1978, he helped the team gain 3,165 rushing yards. This is still an NFL record. In 1986, Hannah helped the Patriots make it to their first Super Bowl.

Mike Haynes DEFENSIVE BACK (1976–1982)

Mike Haynes was the team's first pick in the 1976 **draft**. He became known for his skill as a defensive back and punt returner. Haynes was the first Patriot to score a punt return touchdown.

Andre Tippett LINEBACKER (1982–1993)

Andre Tippett played for the Patriots his whole **career**. In 1985, he helped the team make it to the Super Bowl for the first time. Tippett had 100 sacks during his career. That is more than any other Patriot!

Drew Bledsoe QUARTERBACK (1993–2001)

The Patriots chose Drew Bledsoe as the first pick in the 1993 **draft**. By his second season, he led the NFL in passing yards! Bledsoe helped the team reach the play-offs for the first time in eight years.

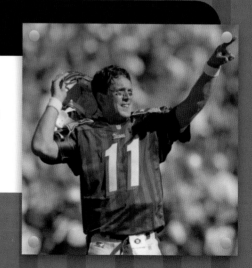

Adam Vinatieri KICKER (1996–2005)

Adam Vinatieri is known for kicking under pressure. He kicked a last-minute field goal to win the Super Bowl in 2002. And, he did it again in 2004! During his **career** with the team, he scored 1,158 points. That is more than any other Patriot!

Tom Brady QUARTERBACK (2000–)

Tom Brady was **drafted** by the Patriots in 2000. He became the team's starting quarterback the next year. He surprised people with his success. Brady led the team to Super Bowl wins in 2002, 2004, and 2005. In 2002 and 2004, he was named the game's MVP.

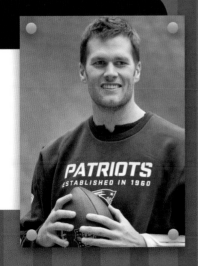

Gillette Stadium

The Patriots play home games at Gillette Stadium. It is in a **suburb** of Boston called Foxborough. The stadium opened in 2002. It can hold about 69,000 people.

Gillette Stadium has a lighthouse and bridge. These were made to remind people of the land in New England.

Merry Minutemen

The Patriots have a **mascot** that is a minuteman called Pat Patriot. Minutemen were American soldiers during the **Revolutionary War**. At home games, Pat Patriot helps fans cheer on their team.

The End Zone Militia also helps cheer on the Patriots. This group stands behind the end zones. They wear costumes from the Revolutionary War.

End Zone Militia members carry old-fashioned guns called muskets. They fire their muskets when the Patriots score!

Running Out the Clock

Minutemen were named for being ready to go to battle at a minute's notice.

Final Call

The New England Patriots have a long, rich history. They won their first Super Bowl in 2002. Then, they led the NFL for most of the next ten years.

Even during losing seasons, true fans have stuck with them. Many believe that the Patriots will remain one of the NFL's greatest teams.

As of 2013, the Patriots had won their division 16 times.

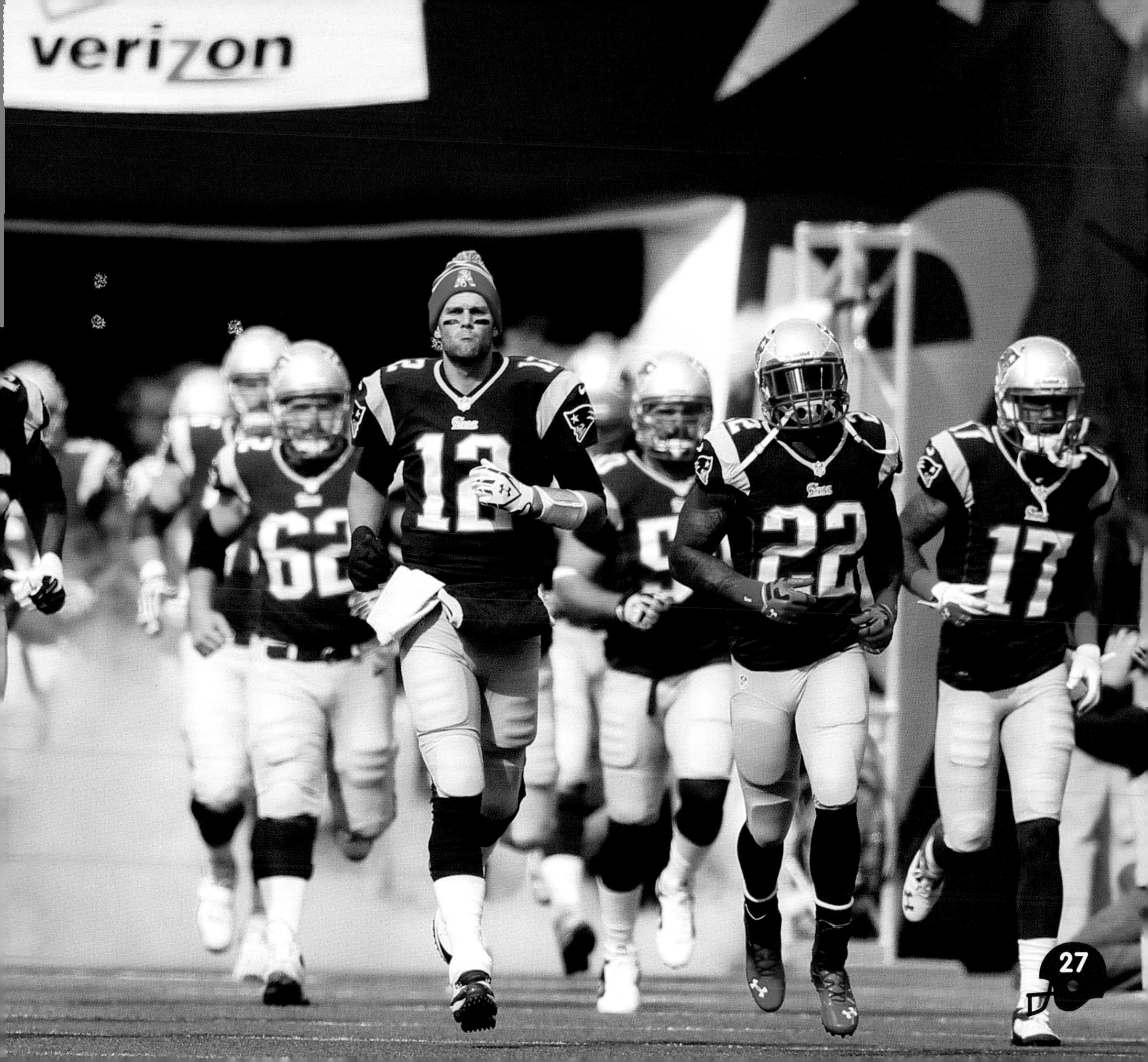
verizon

Through the Years

1986

The Patriots play in their first Super Bowl.

1968

Gino Cappelletti scores more than 1,000 **career** points.

1991

John Hannah becomes the first Patriot in the Pro Football Hall of Fame.

1960

The Boston Patriots play in their first regular-season game on September 9.

1971

The team moves to Foxborough and become the New England Patriots.

1994

Robert Kraft becomes the team's owner. He helps keep the team in New England.

2010

Bill Belichick is named Coach of the Year. He also won the award in 2003 and 2007.

1993

The team gets a new logo. And, their main color changes from red to blue.

2002

The Patriots win their first Super Bowl!

2005

The Patriots win their third Super Bowl in four years.

2007

The Patriots win all 16 games during the regular season.

Postgame Recap

1. Who was the coach of the New England Patriots during their first Super Bowl win?

    A. Drew Bledsoe   **B**. Bill Belichick   **C**. Billy Sullivan Jr.

2. What war is the name and mascot of the Patriots based on?

    A. Revolutionary War   **B**. Civil War   **C**. World War I

3. Name 3 of the 6 New England states that the Patriots play for.

4. Why did the Boston Patriots change their name to the New England Patriots?

    A. The team's owners thought it sounded better.

    B. The Boston Patriots was also the name of a baseball team and they didn't want to confuse fans.

    C. The team moved out of Boston.

Glossary

career work a person does to earn money for living.

championship a game, a match, or a race held to find a first-place winner.

draft a system for professional sports teams to choose new players. When

a team drafts a player, they choose that player for their team.

mascot something to bring good luck and help cheer on a team.

Revolutionary War (reh-vuh-LOO-shuh-nehr-ee WAWR) a war fought between

England and the North American colonies from 1775 to 1783.

suburb a town, village, or community just outside a city.

Websites

To learn more about the NFL's Greatest Teams, visit
booklinks.abdopublishing.com. These links are routinely monitored
and updated to provide the most current information available.

Index